RAGE, RESISTANCE & REDEMPTION

Will To Live.

SIMONE MILLWOOD

A Note from the Author

To the best of my knowledge, there have been only rare occasions, where the humanity of previous generations of people, blessed with dark or dusty hues, have had their experiences channelled into literature.

Channelling a human experience on a level where every person with a compassion, can understand the lived experience of human genius, greatness, hope, pain, and perseverance.

This series of literary works has been created for those whose voices have not been heard were forced to be silent.

My poems are designed to take the reader on a journey that transcends the need to hide from tough and uncomfortable truths. In this place, we can finally share once hidden perspectives and move into a place of grieving, acceptance and then healing.

Table of Contents

FORCEFULLY TAKEN

Forcefully taken upon a bed of lies.
Like a diamond under pressure

      Pressurized under immense weight.

The weight of oppression, its jealousy and lust.
My body convulses.

      Ricocheting with every thrust.

Your breath is putrid.
The stench of your sweat is ripe.

      Clothes are discarded like empty wrappers.

Like a canvas.
My skin is tattooed with marks on your whip.

      Your laugh... echoes.

Under siege, treasures were plundered.
Shame submits to an uncapped greed.

      The bloom of hatred's seed.

Tears fell, teeth gritted.
I closed my eyes.
Time stops.

GUINEAMEN

My mind casts back to home.
Music laughs around the fire... we danced.
Friendly faces float hazily in my mind.

Freewill crowned each step of life-
life was bright as the day once.
Now, accustomed to the dark.

I recall the arrival.
Countless lives reaped.
Harvested like maize,
resisting bodies lay lifeless in heaps.

Rows of chains embrace living limbs,
people numbered; names withheld.
Cattle herded into the bowls of ships.
Souls scream through silent lips.

Cargo packed; humanity shipped,
Black bodies are hidden... the birth of the Guineamen.

From soil, we are created.
Seeds forcefully planted in the depths of seas.
Such a heavy price to pay.

Determined to live free.
They chose to choose.
Such is the privilege of the wise.

THE BLUEPRINT

From his seed,
the spark of life begins.
Strength of the first; encoded in strands of DNA.

Molecular manipulation,
cell multiplication,
blessings, curses, strength and weakness.
Blend in a cacophony of molecular choreography.

His leadership, her mindset,
His Strength, Her nurturing love,
from this, the world of man is sculpted.

From her sacred womb,
life is crafted.
Cosmic force meets blood and flesh.
Encased within, the first beat of man's heart.

BEAUTY

Skin the colour of molasses.
Rich dark browns and dusky hues.
The deepest golden tones
All beautiful.
The colours of the Earth.

Mahogany skin with cinnamon.
From tones of honey.
To burnished brass.
Shades of natural beauty personified.

Skin so deep in hue,
secrets of its beauty;
are yet untold.
Dark skin.

Original Planetary ID,
The mark of the original man,
in pure unmatched glory.
Our beauty glows.

Features compared;
to the heavenly bodies,
where the physical form
is compared to celestial perfection.
Timeless.

ORIGINAL MAN

Eyes dark like rich chocolate,
skin kissed by starlight,
the fabric of the universe,
imagined in human form.

Plump, pillowy lips.
Hair, coiled with love.
And like nature, it rises.
Like the sun, from dawn to midday.

Our strides break boundaries,
builds nations.
Every footstep,
teaches younger generations.

This Sacred womb cradles nations.
We perspire rivers,
life-giving oceans.
Our breasts, like the honeycomb
like hills and valleys.
There is heaven between these slopes.
It flows.

Our lips like the finest mahogany,
smooth and soft to touch.
Our arms protect,
nurturing future leaders,
Amazingly divine.

Deep are the scars,
which tells the lie,
That what is in us, is neither beauty nor life.
Like stretch marks, on the fabric of time,
decimating the flawless background of truth.

As was in the beginning,
so shall it be in the end.
I walk proudly in this undeniable truth,
I am original Man.

IF WE EMBODIED YOUR LIES

If we were truly everything,
you have painted us to be
our communal rage,
would have burnt with such intensity.
Those who are not part of our community,
would have been consumed by the heat of our enmity.

Surely,
We would awake that sleeping Lion,
having finally decided to bare our teeth.
Hungry for the flesh and blood
of the captors of our humanity,
eager to destroy those who rose from our calamity.

We, who are born in many different shades,
could destroy everything in the wake of our rage.
Upon our backs,
you created this modern world.
Under our feet,
it will be crushed without apology.

If we embodied your lies.
There would be no peace,
no fairy tale ending,
Where we all stand united.
Be grateful that;
we do not in any capacity,
embody the lies, so genuinely believed.

LITTLE WHITE LIE

Lies licked across pink lips.
As a little lying tongue clicked,
words weaving as a web of lies.
That would seal the fate of another Black life.

Porcelain skin draped upon a pretty face,
bright eyes in a dark mind.
Told the White males,
those dark hands....
Encircled the waist of a White woman.

Explicit words were exchanged.
Like coins, one offered,
though
transaction declined.
He said yes when she said no.
Or so she sang, as her story unfolds.

Over 4 nights,
2 men with 1 mind.
Planned the abduction.
Of a 14-year-old child.
The accuser who was 21 at the time.

1955, race decided place
White power ruled with an iron fist.
Racism danced upon society's face.
Jim Crow laws fit right into place.

Poverty and power
Place and identity
High rates of Black poverty
Living in a town called Money.

Down south where racism is the only thing hotter than the
chilli.
Where you will receive,
Real, Southern, hospitality.

One night, 2 Men, 1 Child,
Over days, beaten and tortured.
Smashing to a pulp
The child of a proud mother.

Within his head,
a bullet made its bed.
Around his body,
wrapped, barbed wire
Like a demonic present.

His once precious being.
Now empty of the soul,
Thrown into the river.
To float away to be found.

A woman grieved.

As her eyes beheld
The result of hatred unchecked.
And injuries grave
That only a mother's Love
Could be relied upon to recognise her babe.

Such were his injuries.

1 Black life lost.
Due to 1 little White lie.
Some claimed it was a touch.
Some claimed it was a whistle.
Such a minor offence to take a life.

Yet,
Still, the truth remains:

Lies licked across pink lips.
As a little lying tongue clicked,
Words weaving as a web of lies.
That would seal the fate of another Black life.

THE PROMISE.

You promised forever.
With mortal lips.
We fought battles,
facing enemies
back-to-back
Receiving wounds,
Worse than ones left with a sword or spear.
Leaving no mark,
no scars to bear,
but the ones in our soul.

Deeply embedded,
where no surgeon's hand
Could wash clean,
Nor stitch & knit together.
Where pain would stab
No ointment, but time.
We healed each other's wounds.
With the little we had.

When beaten,
I felt your pain.
When our children cried out.
Destroyed.
Their blood cast,
like rabid spittle.
Our organs are traded.
Like stocks and shares.

All too much
For a mother to bear.

My attitude created,
in a harsh climate.
Botheration hidden,
behind smiling faces.
Microaggression,
hidden behind condescending looks.
Selective language,
traversing unhinged characters,
being force-fed,
preferential treatment,
repackaged as
"It's just the way it's done."

Just being,
Is draining.

PERSPECTIVE

Freedom through financial access.
It was a trap!
Something for nothing.
Pretty words and laws
Delicately wrapped.
Tied with bows,
to look appealing.
Yet, our blood is still seeping.

Fear still rife
Atmospheres, so tense
Could be cut with a knife.
Race relations
Taut like an arrow.
Weapons used
to reduce the use
Of an industrious people.

From massacres,
Tar and feathering
Lynchings aplenty.
Drugs vs Ghettos,
Poor schooling,
gangs uplifted.
High incarceration rates,
Welfare induced comas,
Pimping made easy.

In a cruel world of
Preferential treatment,
Rewards and upgrades.
Not seen in dead-end jobs.
Money changes hands,
But always a lack.
Money means nothing.
When the mentality is
No dogs, no Irish, no Blacks!

Economic buck breaking
Tears are hidden behind.
Watermelon smiles.
You better dance, if
You want to move up in life.
Replacing communal strength
For a link to the man
Who was always....
Your final
Destination.

Controlled opposition
Equals in permanent submission.
Animals promoted,
We are being demoted.
Guilty until proven innocent.
Accepted once proven worthy.
Weaponised identity.
Be grateful for the opportunity.

Be less you,
Be more like us.
Smile more.
Why are you so aggressive?
I felt like I couldn't approach you.
Why the attitude?
Can you do this?
Don't you feel appreciated?

You should talk more.
Why so insular?
Smaller, be smaller!
Why?
Just so you can be taller.
Why are your lips big?
Hips broad?
Ass fat?

When we do it, it's ghetto.
When they do it, it's creative.
I'm afraid of you,
But you're the aggressor!
Weaponised tears.
Little white lies
Destroyed more people
Then one thousand diseases.

But everything boils down to perspective.
It always makes a difference.

WHY?

Why is my support expected?
My words accepted,
but only on your terms?
Why is my strength key?
In grim times,
In overcoming suffering,
Yet, insufficient in celebrating?

You would bare your soul and
I would cradle your heart.
Where your decision was never set in stone,
without my advice.
So why?
Though your blood still spills,
Do you find yourself in the arms of those who wish you
harm and death?

If your choice was made solely
on this "newfound" idea of love,
where is your sense of loyalty to look in front of you first?
Why does it take our shape, image and attributes to attract you,
but you still choose counterfeit goods over authenticity?

TO NEVER FORGET

We huddled together,
not knowing
this would be our last meeting.
I cried tears.
Never truly seen.

I grieved for all we were,
all we could have been.
Day and night,
Sadness became our bread.

Beaten and tortured.
I gave you love's healing touch.
I gave you compassion.
I spoke life into your broken existence.

When separated,
My soul traversed the distance,
cried out your name,
I always found your location.

When we worked,
till our fingers bled,
I tore my dress,
for your bandages.
My tears, your balm.
My lips, your cotton.

Upon my back,
lashes licked.
My voice cried out,
my nerves alight,
pain like lightning.

Great welts cascaded upon my temple,
Tattooing trees strong and ample,
With branches great and wide.
Far-reaching.

I covered your body with mine.
My sweat our clothing.
My life's blood running,
Like a mighty river.

I cherished you
Like you were my air
Caught in the torrents
Of human hatred.

I would not part with you
for anything.
You're all I ever wanted.

Head tucked to protect your vitals.
Our defiance,
That needs to be free,
Never broken.
War silently declared.
Left where we were,
it was effortlessly understood.
My strength is your strength.
And your life is mine.

Counted as cattle,
I spoke to you with reverence,
called you by your name and title.
Truth kept alive.
Reflected in tear-soaked eyes.

Our goal;
to stand upon our land,
to once again be free,
rejoice without condition,
speak the tongue of our people.

No matter the time,
no matter the test,
we must always remember
To never forget.

KINDNESS FOR WEAKNESS

Do not mistake my kindness for weakness,
nor my silence for acceptance.
Within me, lurks the power to pull down your walls of lies
and vengeance.

I am not comfortable with the way you think you can,
just because I may be sweet, try to encase me.
In this box of benign condescension, masked as enjoyed
interactions.

Our anger slowly bubbles to the surface and the silent rivers
truly run deep.
I may smile, laugh and effortlessly seem to live.
I will enjoy a laugh or two, while passing away the time.
But wise is the man who catches his prey while wearing the
guise of a foolish mind.

It always astounds me when you think that
I must be part of a system in order to survive,
That somehow, I am happy with the ways of this modern life.
That technology and money rule my life like you are in it to
survive.

We play the part to fit the mould,
but should the chance come,
we would strike with force.
This perceived stalemate would soon be over, and everyone
would know.

How unimportant your presence is and how I dislike you the most.
From your narcissistic behaviour and your sociopathic ways.
Your destructive tendencies,
Embedded deep into your DNA.

Do not mistake my kindness for weakness,
nor my silence for acceptance.
Within me, lurks the power to pull down your walls of lies
and I will repay the past with modern vengeance.

THE SACRED BLACK DIVINITY

I fell in love with our divinity,
from the sacred strength, we are endowed with in unity,
to the preciousness of our virtue and virginity.

I fell in love with our power
that springs forth, spilling over the brim,
anointing our offspring, covering our family.

I fell in love with our patience,
starting as a babbling brook,
progressing into a mighty river,
spreading through our community to many others.

I fell in love with our shine,
emitted from soul, body and mind.
A love that stands the test of pressure, perseverance and
time.

I fell in love with our soul,
that part of us that creates life, language and culture.
Birthing the first teachers, artists, and priests.

I fell in love with our humility,
despite feeling our own pain, we can share ourselves with
others, with uncapped sincerity.

I fell in love with our struggle,
we are greater than the trouble.
For hundreds of years, we strived.
And yet, we are here, alive!

Even in the dark of night, we source the light.
The struggle though the times, is blinding.
Can become the catalyst to us uniting.

I fell in love with our legacy,
though we fight consistently,
From us, great leaders rise and grow endlessly.

I fell in love with our innovation,
we crafted organic technology and improved the human
condition in tandem with nature.

I fell in love with our creativity,
The creation of musical excellence,
That spirit of composition, song and storytelling.

I fell in love with our love.
That spirit that has every other being of life, coming back to
the truth of their origins.

I fell in love with our spirit.
That enables us to be the first and the last.
That spirit that enables us to put forth our DNA and
replenish the earth.

ORDAINED KING AND QUEEN

BLACK MAN
Made from the blueprint of perfection.
Sculpted from glory, mystery, power and cosmic science.
A manifestation of spirit, light, darkness and eternity.
From the lips of wisdom, we are given life and eternity.

Clothed in strength, dominion and authority.
Crowned and ordained for complete superiority.
Life springs forth, wisdom is gained.
Formulas of life, structure and community are built.
Moulded in the fire of opposition, honed by the strength of victory.

In the comfort of your arms,
I feel your silky sweet softness.
The sensation of that ironclad protective embrace
Regardless of time and place.
Reaffirms to me with perfect clarity.

YOU ARE MY PROVIDER, PROTECTOR AND PARTNER.

In the secret of my inner sanctum,
Where time has no power,
Where atoms meet light and eternity,
You are granted lifetime admission.
To learn, to worship and to master and dominate.
To create and recreate life from thoughts, actions and
intensity.

I listen to the steady rhythm of your heart's natural beat.
Like an ancient drum of war.
The sound commands silence and respect within me.
Like a moth drawn to a flame,
Your natural intensity pulls me in.

MY HAIR

Coiled with the precision of a loaded spring,
haloing my head in a thick cloud of wool-like perfection,
adorning it like the most precious crown,
perfecting my complexion with its glory of Black and
Brown.

My hair, my friend and the statement piece to my whole.
The unique element of my glory is unknown.
Unique in every way,
like a tree, my hair grows upwards as if reaching out to the
sun.

Flowing like a lion's mane,
beautiful, free.
This beautiful Afro
is beautifully me.
Like a cord, each strand like an antenna,
provides the connection from me to the divine.

The way my hair can be styled,
whether worn short or long,
flowing gently close to the scalp
or effortlessly down my spine.

From weaving my hair into a plethora of unique styles,
to the plaits that can be made into intricate designs.

My hair, a part of my tribe and identity.
Such a beautiful construction of nature;
strong, wavy, resistant and bouncy.
Thick, lustrous, and soft to the touch.

When opposition to my hair arose,
when cloth was enforced to cover this greatness,
proudly, we wrapped our crowns and made a statement.
Anointing our hair with oils precious and fragrant.

Feathers and flowers were worn, in hair and on turbans,
as statement pieces to maintain our dignity.
We soon structured our hair into the perfect afro.
Confirming our love of self and rejecting the status quo.

From straight to curly or kinky and bold.
Our hair calls forth our freedom and our stories are told.
We love who we are, and all must know.
Oh, how I love this kinky hair that is my afro.

THE SECRET YEARNING

I stand here before you — exposed.
Once safely hidden somewhere, you could not find me.
But life, fate or hope has now given you the key
to see me for who I truly am.
Exposing myself bare will have a lasting effect on me.

I will not ask why, or how, or when, but only if you will be
gentle.
That whatever you say or do from now on, will be done in
reverence.
That every word and every touch will be the lightest,
For I am vulnerable like a new-born child, helpless.

If you ask it of me, I will tell you, my secrets.
I will bare my soul and show you every hurt and regret.
Like a tattoo, each memory is emblazoned upon my chest.

Where all else failed, you have taken the victory.
You have proven that you have what it takes to love and
adore me.
I have waited a millennium for one like you.
My power, my wisdom are yours to use.

I will take a step and cross the chasm of your doubt.
I will pluck the power from your sleeping being and lift you
upon the mount.
I will wrap you in my warm and comforting embrace.
I will lay your head upon my chest and let time fall away.

My spirit longs for your connection.
Your presence has brought light and love to my celestial
direction.
I have found what was lost and all is now well.
For you have brought back the spark in life.
The path that was once closed, now springs forth like a well.

Upon my head, you have placed your crown.
You have heaped upon me, honour and glory once again.
My aura shines like the sun, moon and stars combined.
You have anointed my hands and feet.
You have called forth untold blessings into my life.

You have taken from my hands the weight of the world.
You have reminded me of my sacred duty, and you have
now taken the mantle.
For I am the embodiment of life eternal, you are the vessel
that cleans me anew.
You are the eternal balance, the push to my pull.

For so long, I have waited in the hope that you would come.
I had long forgotten what it was like to walk and live in
love.
You have taken from me the loss of yesterday and filled me
with hope.
That once again I would fulfil the secret of my yearning.

REVOLUTION

Caged, I cried out!
Not caring who hears.
Beating my body against gilded bars,
waiting for someone to let me out.
Or find my battered body.

I look forward, towards the light.
Yet content in the darkness,
constantly waiting, deliberating....
When the best time will be to move.
Watching the time.
Watching the day.
Learning the routine of my captor.

I am determined to be free.... I am determined.

I do not want your food,
it is poison.
My stomach aches
to know that my captor
wishes to prolong my life,
Under their own dominion.
I refuse to eat and would rather take my chances.
I grit my teeth and shut my eyes.
Never showing the depth of my hurt.
I set my face to the sky.
My eyes to the hills.
I realise that to win,
I must play a part.

For time is short and unknown is its length,
like the number of beats in a heart, till ultimate death.
Smile in silence, hide the power!
Frown no longer, groan no more.
We shall fly the flight of freedom,
I must once again soar!

They say poison is as bitter as gall,
but the opposite can be just as true.
For many lose their fight
Survival is not truly the same as living life!
A false sense of comfort or luxury
is the same as simply doing what must be done to get by.
My resistance never rusts, never dulls, never misses its mark.

Smile, and bide your time,
Work towards the goal.
Finding new strengths, working on my weaknesses.
There must be no mistakes.
Walk the path.

Let the bars open and get ready.

Do not feel for the captor,
nor for those who will fall,
as a result of me propelling myself forward.
Caught in the crossfire of wills.
I set myself to the task,
My fist is clenched, ever ready.
My heart is hardened,
my face is set in stone.

I am determined to be free!

I don't want your luxuries,
they are foreign to me.
I would trade sticks and feathers.
For silks and gold.

In the pursuit to be free.
My captors hope to tighten their hold.
They feel justified in capturing body and soul.
Your ways are not my own.

I will break free; I must break free.

The system will make you wonder
if your freedom is still your right.
Then, I remember that I am not part of the system:
my rights are violated.
The best form of respect is acceptance of truth.
So, I await the chance to be rid of this coop.
I play dead, I hear the bars open and my body is lifted.

Arrow straight,
light as a feather, stiff as a board.
Do not let the charade end.
As the tears drop against my skin.
The grip tightens, and I am taken to the door.
It opens.

Like lightning, I arise!
Dive-bomb my captor,
scratch and peck the eyes.
In the ensuing chaos,
I take my chance!
I fly through the window, without a second glance,
take flight like the eagle, soaring high to the skies.

Show me your fear.
I shall show you, my love.
I look down from my height
My captor's eyes fill with shock.
I hear the call of the need to be free.
I answered the call.
Freedom is what I need.

HANGING FRUIT

The whining,
that high-pitched sound
permeating intermittent calm.
Like a lazy beat,
determined not to repeat.
On time.

The ropes with an iron grip.
Coiled around trees
like a snake leisurely sleeping-
immovable and contrasting.
The rope binds its fruit to the tree.

Such fruit,
heavier than a tree should bear.
Yet, always ripe.
Every precious burden
in an endless dance.
Rope swinging,
its fruit motionless.

The sun hits the fruit,
ripening further its flesh.
Birds circling, pests waiting.
Eager for a taste.

The orchards boast trees,
all in varying states
of bearing.
Some fruit struggle,
but all still hang.
Heavy laden.

New fruit is selected.
The rope coils ever tighter,
Earth nor the sky can help.
The newest arrivals.
New fruit must ripe,
this is the season.

Fruit selected,
tree prepared,
grouped hands:
Heave Ho!
A unity so coordinated.
The burden is hoisted effortlessly.

Fruit placed.
centre stage.
Hands and feet tied,
mouth twisted,
eyes bulge
till centre stage.
The fruit waits to ripe.

The fruit moves,
the dance of death,
vibrating shudders,
ripples through branches.
Leaves dance crazily
like tassels.
A murderous chorus
continued the tails of the wind.

Hanging bodies,
once filled with life.
Now hollow husks,
eyes vacant,
limbs a mixture
of stiff and relaxed.

No fear,
or love,
mind or hand,
can return
what was taken!
The tree is a living testament.

The only beating hearts are
The ones left behind.
All looking up.
some laughs,
others simply watch.

What manner of man
creates such produce?
So, approving of its brand.
Souvenirs are made of the very rope
that disposed of life.

A feast for the eyes.
Sometimes human lips.
Such an exquisite taste,
created for acquired palates.
Delicate morsels alight
excited tastebuds.

A picnic event in many places
where whoops and shouts
followed each burden.
A man or woman.
Children of varying ages...

Condemned to death
before life has judged.
Now no more chances
to be among living souls.
What a strange thing to see.
Unripe fruit from the flesh of humanity.

THE CARBON PLEDGE

I am limitless.
There is nothing that I cannot do.
I walk with my head held high.
I walk with the power of countless generations.
I fear nothing and no one.
My life is my own.
I have a responsibility to my community.
I am them, and they are me.
We are one sacred entity.

I am the protector, the guardian, and the teacher.
My mother, my sister,
My wife, and my daughter,
I cherish.
They are all expressions of who I am.
My father, my brother,
my husband, my son, and my people,
Legacies of power, glory, perfection, and wisdom.
One helps another, we all rise together.
Brother helps brother.
Sister helps sister.
We rise, we grow, and we build together.

RAGE, RESISTANCE & REDEMPTION

I am made perfectly.
I am worthy.
I am respected.
I am cherished.
I am never alone.
I will not be brought down.
I will not be disrespected.
I accept my shortcomings and change accordingly.
We build together.
I learn from the past.
I own the future.

This is my pledge, my promise and my goal.

WHEN THE HEAD IS BOWED

Impure hands placed on a pure body,
defiling soul, mind, and spirit,
the raw pleasure gained through the hand of domination,
an Infidel's desire to oppress a royal nation.
For whom the bell tolls, time will surely tell.

The deconstruction of kingdoms,
The abdication of the Golden Throne,
The disconnect and disrespect of the head of the home.
No more glad tidings, or the support.
The structure is now gone,
the greatness is forgotten and only a void remains.

The shake and rhythm of time-honoured tradition,
natural skills, talent, knowledge, and wisdom.
All are hidden in a locked basement.
Caged in the minds of dead generations.
Unable to pass the knowledge on,
locked in the power of a closed grave,
if there is one truth, it's dead men tell no tales.

Heavy is the head that wears the crown.
But which king can be respected if his head is bowed?

LONGING

If I could close the miles between us,
I would reach into the pages of your soul,
most carefully and read your story, as I caress the pages.
I wish to read the impossible and learn more about you.
Aspects of your character, you never even knew.
I would search your contents, and read from the first page
to the last.

I would learn what makes you unique.
I would memorise your deepest yearnings
and fulfil each over time and throughout eternity.
I would read your regrets and dry your secret tears.
I would heal your wounds and speak life into all your
broken places.
To calm the storms of life that, inside you, rages

If I could close the miles between us,
I would traverse great distances to reach you.
The unspoken words of my soul would embrace you.
Pulling you irresistibly to my direction.
Words too sensitive to speak would be shown to you in
telepathic clarity.
Reverently touch the spaces hidden within you.

THE TRUTH

From the curve of my hips,
Humanity was given the rite of life.
Upon my breast, you suckled nature's milk.
In screams of pain and anguish.
You were brought forth.
Manifested from months of hope.
As you now find sleep upon my chest.

Snuggled against my heat within the curve of my arms,
Listening wistfully to the sound of my heartbeat.
Remembering your time within me.
Child of creation, thrust into the light of the world,
With vibrant sound, mixed with man's conflict and Ever-
changing attitudes.

I watch you, content, speaking the word of life to you.

From that beautiful halo of Afro
Framing your head in sacred reverence
I let my fingers touch your infinite curls
Proud of my creation and my gift to the world.
Hearing your little sounds as you sleep, I caress you Gently.
My eyes follow the curves and planes of your face,
from your beautiful eyelashes laid against chocolate Skin
To your perfectly sculpted button nose, placed Delicately in
the middle.

Examining all the places where you took my features, now yours.
Counting your fingers and counting your toes.
Seeing family long passed in your features,
I know that within you, lies the hidden truth of Generations.
I stare at you in wonder, knowing that you are mine,
Wanting to keep you safe,

This divine responsibility is mine.

From my past to your future,
Upon your shoulder, this child carries, my hope.
That they will move forward upon my prayers.
To accomplish feats my mind could not conceive.

My kisses bless you
My cuddles protect you
My heart is yours
Never knowing that, until now
My life lacked the encompassing meaning
Provided by your presence.

IT IS NOT A CRIME

As a race of people who have gone through so much,
we never had the chance to simply recover and just stop.
Stop doing, stop fighting, stop having to prove
that we have just as much right to live in this world.

We have been tolerated, castigated, separated, and
dominated.
We have been used, abused, evaluated, devalued and still, it
is of no use.
We are here to stay, for we are the first instance of man.

We have been made to sit when we are a people
That stands!
We have been dehumanised to build up the rest of
humankind.
We have been forced to "Kneel" for a terrible beast.
We have been made to eat crumbs from tables we built and
created.

So, excuse me if we are not as organised as the rest.
Excuse me if we do not meet the criteria for your human test.

We are too busy most times, simply trying to just live.

When we rise as a people, it is deemed as a threat.
Whether non-violent or in protest, we are deemed as
terrorists.
But it takes one to know one!
Til this day, why are the KKK labelled as a Christian
organisation, but the Black Panthers are painted as a gang
of thugs?

Remember Black Wall Street and where they were based?
Remember what atrocities were committed to take over that
space?
The burned-down houses, bullet-riddled corpses,
mowed down for being prosperous and independent only.

It is not a crime to speak out against the violence of the police.
It is not a crime to want to rebalance your mind.
It is not a crime to focus on the things that make you
different.
It is not a crime to love your people and want your own
healthy family.

It is not a crime to want to break the society, that has
caused so much pain.
It is not a crime to point the finger in their direction, to
show who is to blame.
It is not a crime to want to reject the lies that have been
said.
It is not a crime to control your voice, your story and your
narrative.

MANHOOD

Don't you realise how important you are?
Don't you know how much you are needed?
You have no limit, you are unstoppable.
Even when it feels like it, you are never alone.
For you are greater than the powers of the world.
So, build yourself up from the inside out.

There is no one greater than you.
Expect and call forth what you want, and it will come to you.
Cry when you need to, hide when you must.
Believe in yourself and be someone that others can trust.

Feel completely,
but do not be ruled by your feelings.
Do not hide your hurt!
Every emotion you have is valid.

Clothes do not define you,
money does not define you.
You are a magical being.
You are the most essential element in life.

Keep walking, hold your head up high,
for you are royalty and you are amazingly divine.

WOMANHOOD

You are more than your hairstyle.
You are more than the way you look.
You are mightier than a sword.
You have more impact on life than the pen.

Love yourself entirely and let no one tear you down.
Recover from every setback and rise again.
Cry when you need to, but do not stay down.
Heavy is the head that wears the mighty crown.

You are a success story to someone out there.
Your life is a beacon of light to many lost in life's storms.
Aim high and be careful with whom you share your time.
Time is a precious commodity, something you cannot reclaim.

Do not rush to be seen,
take your time to develop.
Enjoy the process and rise to the highest levels.
Walk with your head held high, let no one stop you.
Believe in no limits because you are naturally limitless.

Respect your body and protect it at all costs.
You are the future bearer of the next generation, and they must not be lost.
You are a precious being, take pride in yourself.
You are someone to be praised, understood, and cherished.
You do not have to compete to show you have merit.
There is no one like you in this entire world, so find a way to live your truth and take this world by storm.

Your capacity is limitless.

THE PRINCE'S POEM

Young prince, look at yourself in the mirror.
Look at your beauty and know that you are powerful.
Let no one take your confidence.
Or tell you lies about yourself and your people.

Face your fears head-on
And take your time in defeating each one.
Do not crumble under the pressure,
Life will be hard, but you are strong.

Ignore negative remarks and words,
No matter who speaks to them, be it a friend, family or Foe.
Tell yourself daily that everything in this world is yours.
Even if you make a mistake, from it you can learn.

Open your heart to the possibilities within you,
Take care of your mind and protect your body.
Be wise in all things, and learn how to depend on Yourself
and your community.

Love with caution, truth and without illusion,
Speak out against injustice, and stand up for your People.
Protect yourself!
For you are precious.
You are not alone, and you will always be supported.

On your shoulders, you carry great weight.
Do not be stopped by the burden, continue to run your Race.
There will be times when you feel that you can't go on,
But you must
Gather your strength and move forward.

THE PRINCESS POEM

Young princess, look at your beauty.
You are stunning, you are graceful,
from your head to your feet.
You are the epitome of divinity.

You are delicate and from this, you gather strength
to walk with authority and achieve greatness.
Your tears are precious and a secret language to power.
Your ability to love blooms endlessly like an infinite flower.

Diamonds and Gold cannot compare to you.
Your image and wisdom are the basis of all beauty and truth.
Dainty and effortlessly stunning,
from your ability to enhance clothing,
to the way you stand out in a crowd.

Embrace your hidden depths and free your mind.
Protect your precious heart and still be tough,
compete with no one.
Your own abilities are unique and enough.
Take advice from the right people, be grounded and
gracious to those you meet.

Feel every emotion and hold back from hate.
You are a vessel of love and that makes you great.
Look at yourself and declare only positive things.
Explore your power and what lies hidden within.

Young princess, focus your mind on good things,
not just the clothes on your back.
Take your face from your phone and instead read a book.
For this life is a net and its lies are the hook.

HUMAN

Tears fell from her eyes,
she beheld.
Innocence-incarnate within her hand.
Through storms of pain
as contractions wave,
rippling pain and power
to bring for her babe.

Eyes roaming this wonder,
precious treasure.
Marvel of life,
so young and so tender.
New-born cries float to her ears.
A reminder to the world that she was here.
Pain forgotten,
she stares anew.
Deep brown eyes, so bright and new.

Eyes sparkling,
awareness keen,
brow furrowed,
blood still clings to him.
Baptised in water,
created in love.
From springs of water, her seed is grown.

A prince yet unnamed,
As he suckles still tired
skin.
Still, within this joy comes the fear,
when this child no longer bears
the chubbiness of childhood and grows into a man.

When the child is too big
for his mother's hand.
When he treads upon this world's land.
Temptation,
provocation,
oppression he will taste.
Who will protect his life, many may wish to erase?

But until this time.
Locked inside,
the ills of this will, she will hide.
Safely cradled in the crook of her arm.
Three hearts now beat as one.
The mother, the father and their beautiful young son.

Welcome, young human to this world.

DO YOU SEE?

Eyes of darkest brown,
coffee-coloured richness.
Tell me through those beautiful orbs,
where your power lies.
The secrets of your magnetic orbit.
We gaze in wonder.
All who gather,
travel around these eyes.
Like the sun, they shine!

Those bountiful lips,
smooth and soft to the touch,
pillowy and perfectly balanced,
full to the brim with natural delights.
Be careful!
These lips cradle both life and death.
Power to calm the seas of man,
to weather life's storms,
Tempered with just one word.

Those curves,
so deliciously served!
With attitude to match.
See her hips move to a beat,
far older than time.
From waist to hip, every rise and dip,
tempered, refined,
these hips can send the civilised, wild.
Wars have been fought for this.

Thighs shapely,
upon solid and smooth legs.
These thighs, thickly made,
padded with generations of untapped power.
Wrapped in glorious colour.
to have them:

An honour.

How could I not speak on this bounty?
Width, breadth,
height and circumference
of her buttocks.
Sweet dreams are made of this.
Men traversed air,
land and sea,
to feast their eyes
on such a natural delight.

Gravity-defying,
refused to be bowed.
Lifted like worship.
Every strand,
coiled like a tensioned spring,
emerge it will,
softer than cotton,
harsh like wool,
woven in genetic mystery.
Magically coiled to form.
A halo that frames the face.

Eyes are drawn to it.
Fingers fly like superheroes.
Begging to bask in it.
It's so soft,
it smells so good.
It's so frizzy,
a perfect combination.

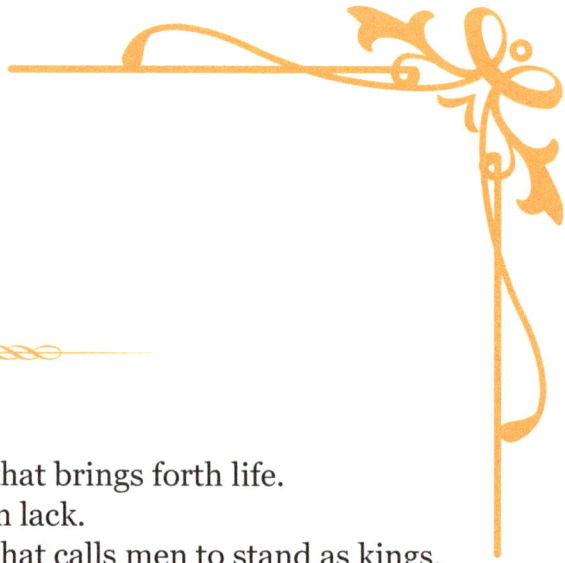

MY BLACK

My Black is the type of black that brings forth life.
My Black breeds abundance in lack.
My Black is the type of black that calls men to stand as kings.
My Black rocks Earth and makes Heavens shake.

My Black is the type of black that turns red lips peach and
blue eyes brown.
My Black empowers the mind to tear corrupt governments
down.
My Black is the type of black that exposes lies.
My Black is the type of black that reveals what is hidden in
plain sight.

My Black is the type of black that is the master file.
My Black multiplies one into many.
My Black is the type of black that is written in space and time.
My Black bends the light and calls in the dawn.

My Black is the type of black that loves to explore.
My Black whips up hurricane and storm.
My Black is the type of black that awakens sleeping minds.
My Black can withstand weapons of war.

My Black is the type of black that is untouchable, unsinkable,
irresistible, and immovable.

That is the type of Black that I am!

IF I DID TO YOU WHAT YOU DID TO ME

If we tied up your family like common cattle,
corralling them into restricted spaces for Preparation,
to be sold at auction, no more valuable than the meat on
their bones.
Paraded and forced to perform.
If we tore your children from your arms,
could we still be called human beings?

If we took your women against their wills,
forced them to bear their enemies' children.
Bound their hands and their minds.
Whipped trees of burden into their very backs,
hung them, tarred, and feathered them,
whilst calmly watching from the audience,
what would you honestly think of us?

If we used your hair to fill our chairs and pillows,
used your skin to create clothing and delicate purses.
If we even had the habit of placing our people into vats of
boiling sugar,
as punishment for whatever sin,
would you believe in human justice?

Imagine us taking the ones you cared for,
selling them to others, with no mention of where their
destination lies.
Over years of sorrow, wondering if they were dead or alive.
Forced to work in the oppressive rays of the hot sun.
Made to eat the leftovers from the ones who hate you.
Wouldn't you want to be free, and your pain expressed?

If we had done to you, what was done to us.
If we had done to you, what continues under the cover of
disguise.
What would be your next move?

HIDDEN IN PLAIN SIGHT

I am the roots that run through your veins.
I am the ancestors you venerate.
I am the blueprint of your DNA.
I am the face you seek to hide.
I am the darkness you cover with light.
I am the power you seek to control.
I am the ending you wish to run from.

Because I am, you are!

My blood spilled like a libation.
My image distorted through generations.
My knowledge was polluted to hide realisation.
My lessons were removed to indoctrinate future generations.
All in the quest for world domination!

I am the strength you wish to harness.
I am the power you wish to tarnish.
I am the truth you wish to change.
I am the history you dare to rearrange.
I am the first you want as the last.
I am the peace you will never have.
I am the Science, the Art, and the Form.
I am the truth hidden in plain sight.

DO NOT

Do not shed tears for me,
when you sat idly by,
as bruises kiss my face,
my mind and my psyche.

Do not bow the knee,
if it is not done knowingly,
understanding what it truly means,
and why it is important to bow.

Do not fight for me,
if you only see
dollar signs and money.
Dismissive of my people,
whilst accepting the mockery of our humanity.

Do not pretend to understand,
when you are part of the problem
by being silent, by downplaying,
by casually dipping your feet in torrid waters.

Depending on how you feel,
depending on who you are with,
telling truth, rebuking others...

Yet doing nothing to change things.

I cannot turn off who I am
on a whim.
I am still the same yesterday, today, and tomorrow.
You cannot fight for Me
if you are more concerned with how it will seem.

Do not think you are so selfless
that you are faithful to the cause,
different from those before you,
ingrained and old habits die hard.

The ever-present need, to be in the role of master.
Whether seen or silent, can only lead to disaster.
Unifying on your terms, whilst expecting all to follow.
Not realising your direction is wrong and its support renders
hollow.

The expectation to speak in spaces, where you should be
silent.
Clueless of the obsession to be always in the centre.
The option of accepting your often intrusive involvement.

That ever-present fear
Of no longer holding the strings.
Whether it be by the purse, or by the life.
That fear of relinquishing control to "lesser" beings.

BLACK GOLD

Skin the colour of burnished brass,
richer than coffee and the cocoa bean.
Just as fertile and life-giving as the darkest soil.
Bronzed to perfection, such a beauty to behold.

Crafted in divine fires, sculpted with the greatest materials.
Power, Beauty, Dominion, Peace and honour are the right,
given to all who share the qualities of original humankind.

Planetary ID in melanated glory.
Created from supreme intent, vibration, and energy.
Woven with the magnificence of stars,
Oh, how wonderful are the calculations of God!

We are Jewels in human form, great beings to behold.
Calm as a summer's day or as violent as a winter's storm.
Walking the earth with majesty.
All who see them, bow in awestruck captivity.

From all civilisations made, the royal root will always be
Black Gold.

THE ART OF PAIN

Pain,
Which flows like blood.
The type of pain that transforms,
turning peaceful to violent,
from outspoken to silent.
Pain that drains joy from the soul,
muscle from bone.
Weight is shed like melted butter,
pain that dislocates.
Mind and heart.

Pain which cradles sickness,
twisting veins and sinews.
Limiting quality of life.
Pain that breaks character,
turning Alpha to Omega.
Pain that makes a giving heart,
turn to stone.
Pain which breaks you,
bringing to the knees,
great men, women and families.

RAGE

Damn right, I am angry,
I am enraged.
For too long
our pain has been left to fester.
Oozing with yellow pus.
Injuries torn open
leaving rotting infection
down to the marrow
of the bone.

Like a foul smell,
it follows us.
Your contempt.
Always watching,
like the beast of the field.
The disbelief!
That we dared to keep living.
That must be it!

Still 1/5 a human
without having to say it
'cause that would cause issues.
Financial strains.
So, let's keep it secret!

My women dying at prominent levels;
in childbirth and pregnancy,
not being believed
when we say;
WE FEEL PAIN!
Support is given if we want to
put away the men in prisons.
Isn't that something?

How to say clearly
that YOU are not one of US
without it being obvious.
Shareholders would not be happy
with a financial dip.
Remember, in all things,
the investment must be protected.

Long ago, our pain
was used as a symbol to understand
the needs of all.
Other ideas added to what was supposed to be ours
till their agenda became more important,
breaking away.
Alongside it went funding.
In its place meagre support, and a lack of understanding
till we became a side note
in the chapter of our own story.

All these buzzwords.
Diversity.
Inclusion.
Equal opportunities.
Underrepresented
All negative to me
BME
BAME
When all we want is a pot for just us.
All other communities have the same.

Want to hear a joke?
Even those who support,
rarely have an identity.
So really, there is no real independence
to highlight who we are
for a few days in a month.

Just given a limited-budget
to help a struggling community.
Give a man a fish,
He will eat for a day.
Teach him how to Fish,
He will eat for a lifetime.

But the rage I feel,
stems from having to even say these words
and experience these things.
If our independence is reliant on surviving.
That is the difference...

JOY

Your smile transforms a room
with no effort at all.
You capture attention.
Eyes are called to you, simply drawn.

Your entrance is like a cool zephyr,
which refreshes mind, body, and soul.
Ignoring you is not an option.
You are meant to be seen. Unequivocally.

The envy of others,
so brilliantly you shine.
In a world of presence,
you are simply divine.

That confidence, that aura.
That quiet unchartered power.
That shine of your essence.
Like a morning dew's shower.

Whether Man or woman, girl, or boy,
shine your sweet light!

Show all your joy.

A SONG OF REGRET

The fight,
Forgotten are the dates that signified its start.
Yet ongoing in its pace,
with no clear victory on any side.

Endlessly tired,
are the bystanders, who watch a silent war.
Wondering why, how, and when it started,
what was the reason, what was the cause?

Ceasefire!
Dreaming, when now the stakes are raised,
Russian roulette, playing life-defining games.
Where life is wagered, like chips on a checkboard stage.

Who suffers?
The ones left behind,
silent whispers of judgement,
tears anointing flower-covered paths.

Another young life taken.
Whether RIP or HMP,
where your absence is missed,
by the ones who loved you first.

RAGE, RESISTANCE & REDEMPTION

Silently staring at beige ceilings.
The only smile is bitter.
Its coldness, restricts its natural warmth.
Where days and nights are counted,
when they left or when they returned.

Trapped,
in the cycle of power vs powerlessness.
Where opinions are artfully painted
to complete a warped narrative.

Too busy with the goal of human survival,
guardians lose focus
in the cost-of-living debacle.
Watchful guidance losing in the heat of struggle.

Cycles!
Too many alternating,
wound into each other, undulating.
Where what ifs and What could bes
are captured like butterflies in nets.

Scream!
Where hopes and dreams
are consumed in the fire of bad choices.
The damage stark, no matter life's balm and bandages.

About the Author

Simone Millwood is a London creative.

Simone credits her creativity to the amazing vibrancy of her Jamaican heritage.

This heritage has encouraged her love of expression and creativity through the Arts, fuelling an insatiable love of all things dramatic, sensational and amazing.

Simone is also a philanthropist and is currently opening a charitable organisation called the Verna Mae Foundation in October 2025, which will provide scholarships, bursaries and aid to students living below the poverty line in the Caribbean and will expand to countries within Africa.

Simone is currently putting the perfecting touches on her 2nd Collection of poems called:

"Putting Into Words the Unspeakable."

This anthology of poems explores the Black experience of emotions, the abuse we suffered, mental health issues, depression and all the elements of life that society finds hardest to accept, express and explore.